Diverse Voices from Ireland and the World

Hex/PaulBregazzi

Hex Poems' Awards

"Trajectory" took second place in *Magma Journal* editor's award, UK.

"Woodcock" was highly commended in the Francis Ledwidge Poetry Awards.

"October laneway" was shortlisted in Touchstone Haiku Awards, US.

"Tearaways" took 3rd place in Poems for Patience, Galway.

"Tree" was shortlisted for the Bridport Prize, UK.

"Dipper" was shortlisted in The Rialto/RSPB Nature Poem Competition, UK.

"Goldfinch" won the Cúirt New Writing Award, Galway.

Hex

Paul Bregazzi

Published in 2023 by
Salmon Poetry
Cliffs of Moher, County Clare, Ireland
Website: www.salmonpoetry.com
Email: info@salmonpoetry.com

ISBN 978-1-915022-40-0

Cover Image by *Sally Caulwell, illustrator. sallycaulwell.com*
Cover Design & Typesetting: *Siobhán Hutson Jeanotte*

Printed in Ireland by Sprint Print

Salmon Poetry gratefully acknowledges the support of
The Arts Council / An Chomhairle Ealaíon

In memoriam

Mam, Dad, Ursula,
Nan and Grandad,
and all the old crew

Contents

Hoard

We piled
poem fragments
stones
tickets
trinkets and feathers
a sedimentation of meaning

Now we retrieve it
holding up fragments of shadow days
shades of flagrant nights
an archaeology of love.

14 Ways to Eat a Poet

Quickly, with starved bites or sniffingly,
daintily, unsure if they aren't past their best.

Quaff her, freshly pressed, *New Yorker* style,
later snack on her in the caff.

Take a nibble behind your *Hello!* on a gaberdine wet train
or have him in your pocket for some surreptitious dipping.

Lie back depressing summer grasses, hold her
overhead, then ruminate her through the day.

Their oeuvre your *smorgasbord*,
your lips smacked round their plosives.

His diphthongs your *amuse-bouches*,
his syllables your syllabub.

Comfort-eat someone's *'Collected'*
after days of rain and heartache;

tuck your bib in, loose your waistband,
for a slap-up *gorgepoemfest*.

Trajectory

Mr Hennessy was in full
flight in Friday double maths
and his uniform line of 'this'll be useful
when yous are on the buildings in Frankfurt'

was still hanging in the air when a green-finned dart thudded into his sum

he looked at it for the time it took
his Adam's apple to rise and fall
then his arm took off like some
elegant bird into his calculation

Woodcock

A thump on the classroom window
breaks the mood; learning is lost as we raggle-taggle
out the fire doors. Below the sill, the tawny ball rolls
in a wind of its own. Buff underfeathers flurry,
showing the eyelid-skin breast, the tripod of legs and bill.
The gimlet gob draws gasps as the wild flickers
in the jet of its eye.

Now, the wounded wood kerne is borne towards our world,
held high above the child horde following the spoil,
wings over-lapped, to safen it from us.
But on our threshold, it explodes towards its sky —
leaving us askance.

October laneway
a planetarium
of fallen apples

Care Taker

for George Lawler's retirement

First in, last out,
He swings great steel gates,
Drags and hauls huge wheelie-bins,
Wrestles chair-stacks through the door.

He is the wonder of the boys,
On the roof or on the mower,
Or behind the double doors,
Where the boiler purrs and bubbles.

Then he shepherds small ones in a line,
Places in their hands
Papery bulbs or timely seeds
So they follow in his footsteps,

Begging brushes in the autumn
For the sweeping of the fall.
He talks harvest words to them,
Wraps himself round trees for them,

Throws ash keys to the future.
The air vent in the old school gable
Whistles out his starling words.
Leaves fall at his leaving.

Neighbourhood

Legend

The ground slopes slowly in the direction of the river flow.
Underfoot, reclaimed silt and clábar.
The air carries meat-factory reek of bone meal,
watery shit from skidding cattle.

Two black widows

They crank out the comics
from behind a fly-blown window,
their black nails clicking in the change.

Laneway

From the half-door's unknown dark
seep smells of cabbage and prayers.
He plies his trade
in fishy disdain,
loose cigarettes, lead-weighed potatoes,
a limp of vegetables.

Slump

Fenian Street;
down it came
de-tenanted tenament,
a blanket of brick
for two small girls.

Tears solidified
into an open-armed white Christ,
his back to the modern flats

while the pipes
in the basement sewers
went on weeping.

Once in Dublin

'Small things / Make the past / Make the present seem out of place.'
EAVAN BOLAND *Once in Dublin*

In a crooked rag ball at the foot of the basement stairs
Mary Loobey, *wino*, drinker of Red Biddy,
once of this parish. A black pool
by her head, dried into the last step.

Forty Coats, of the tribe of unfortunates
and knockabouts, trailing
a waft of rags in his wake. Pushing through
with the jangle of his tyreless bike.

The Wanderer, seven foot branch in his fist
striding from Northside to Southside
hair aflame, his eyes
dancing in the maelstrom.

Discarded clothing in the Lotts, sleek black from laneway gutters,
coated with grease from restaurant back doors.
By plywood exits leaving in layers,
the ends of them buckled in rain.

Christmas in Rome

Few the signs of glitter or baubles on the cracked city streets,
where the beggar woman walks waist bent, face to ground.

Just the crib dioramas of shepherds and stall keepers,
lit houses and huddled forms of the cardboard people under the aqueduct.

No donkeys, but the marque of the black horse on the roaring red car
and the man near Termini Station bedding down

with his bike with the girl with her dog with the sign 'we hunger'.
In the Museo Palatino, two pristine wings of an angel, bereft of body.

Later, beset by a beggar's wild infernal face, I turn and bellow *basta!*

Basta: enough

Breaking Bottles at the Old Men's Shelter

Francis bends over tea-chests of cullet
pick and throw pick and throw
his back broadened by his broadcoat
his grizzled head turtles from his collar

he is here in crud and old fear regardless
drink cakes the corners of his mouth
his lined hands pause in their picking
pinch tobacco threads from his lips

rummage in the depths of his shellcoat
surface with a cockle-paged notebook
he mooches in it with his bookies pencil
reburies it in his undergrowth

he shambles down the yard now for tea
the yard end his terminus
some Greek hero in a long travail

Vessel

i.m. Alan Ruddock
(merchant seaman, teacher, martial artist)

Your collar was fraying
through and through.
The fibres slowly giving
way; warp unwefting
unseen, the tiny
threaded
fibres
untwist,
release inbuilt tensions.
Strand by strand the undoing
gains
until
one day you stretch yourself —
the vessel lurches slightly.
It gives

and you are underway.

dark cathedral
stars on the floor
sparrow droppings

Stinkhorn

Phallus impudicus

It rises from the turf of veined pine needles;
the knob — slick and fly stuck — seeps
the reek of some thing, putrifying.
Each near step pumps the fetid scent
of breeze over a slumped carcass.

Close by, the tumbled *claí* cushioned in moss
draws up battle wounds packed with sphagnum,
medieval holes wiped with wads of dripping
coolness from the hills, the smell of bog and prick
of needle still in it — the single wild note
in the miasma of the *civium*, hot waft
of the just-thrown night soil,
shake of the last drops
from the night's small ale.

From these hills above the Dubh Linn,
from *bothóns* in the runoff under the trees,
from bit-hiss in the fire, the cold
heat of damp branches,
see them bring down; slipping
on the black buttery peat, hauling
on slidecars; tinder, coney pelts, ouzel
and jenny wren, coltsfoot and hart's tongue,
whins, puffballs
and stinkhorn.

Valentine

You are my bouquet
of blackberries
white fingers tipping, tipping,
holding,
taking root
without release.

The perfect curves
of your thorns,
each a back-word
facing hook
catching, dragging,
weal on cicatrice.

Soon comes low hanging fruit:
hard green, fire
red to deepest black.

Till
at your ripest
a worm in the blood
there is no turning back.

Nervous Breakdown

The boy sits on the return
of the stairs, just out of sight from below,

a magpie feather in his hand. He rolls
the shaft between his fingers — until

a sheen of purple green catches. A whiffle
of dressing gown from the foot of the stairs

and his name called.

But he claws the carpet to lift himself
a step higher, waits for the hole in space

to become the sound of a ball-bearing
in the living room door. He releases his grip

and his breath. With the wind-blade in his hand,
he conducts the air on the stairway, then

places it in his hard-covered notebook,
tapes it down, mouths the magpie's measures.

Tucked in

on their horsehair mattress
with the blue ticking
at the top of the narrow stairs
in their Corporation house in Drimnagh;
Granny and Grandad.
In a fug of age he had become
his greasy hat and tobacco 'tache.
She, held together
by her bursting floured apron.
Sometimes, and we sent to bring them tea,
she would shoo us children out,
fuss over him, cosset him.
On a day he made it downstairs
we might rifle the wardrobe
to handle his embroidered belt
from the great War.
Or play house with the sickroom
set. The silver paten,
the small Christ — hanging resigned
on his cross of gilt and ebony,
two sconces,
crystal bowls for water
and chrism. All the fittings
for a good death.

Carrying my Father

We lifted my father
to the toilet,
my mother and I.
He hung between us
like his old dressing gown.

Afterwards,
weeks, months, I'd bury
my head in it,
on the back of his door,
inhaling what little breath
he had left.

Hex

I hex the pallid grave with a rosary
wrought of silver from jackdaws' eyes

an armour of leg bones
scaled, springy and giving

a cloak of ebony wings
against the night fall

a gorget of arrowed tongues
for the nit picking

for nib a beak
black blood the ink

Petrichor

You sit in the waiting line or room
mahogany seat chipped handrails
the sea-coloured terrazzo floor
its brass inlay dull
no sunshine lights this far corridor
Posters
more detail than you can take in
jolly graphics of gastric corruption
coronary gunkpipe
how to wash your hands
ask us to wash our hands
ask us to hold your hand
you wait ten twenty thirty
minutes past your appointed time
each door opened
changes your heart rate
each rustled file or rising slow name call
not you
you drop into reverie
and suddenly
you are called
into the presence
— damp out — could be better
— now —
let's — see — ah — yes — so —

and moments later
you are outside
breathing it in

nesting time —
the magpie returns
the branches to the tree

Sanctuary

We drove that day along the Highlands coast
headed north.
Clouds moving out over the Atlantic
threatening.
Sunlight threw darts through
the missed
opportunity. The longer the gap went on
the harder
it got to close.

A bump in the road and the glovebox
flies open. We stare at its silent mouth.

The sun hits the gannets as they
throw themselves
at the sprat-life below.
'Ailsa Craig!' she shouts.
We grasp the short joy
of the nominative. Sigh
around the next bend
away from the accusative.

Delicate Negatives

My father had brittle pictures
of light-drawn ghosts,
preserved in mouldering boxes
of mottled cardboard
were glass photographic negatives
of vanished tramcars,
obsolete omnibuses,
taken when they were still
due the respect
of their full title.

As children we were
allowed to look at these
treasures of light captured on glass,
sometimes to handle them.
Always that sense
of something strange,
being given.

Not of this time,
nothing spoken,
but an inkling of something
precious
that was in our possession.
Allowed to hold them,
we would lift them with reverence,
aware of their sharp edge,
unaware how deep it would cut.

Higgs Boson

Such a small thing to be God
and so hard to find

that messages ring the world
and even little ones
smaller in their world
than any boson
acclaim the finding.

These are the small ones
who slow the others
who move them
to collide usefully
to bang big.

Morning High Above Bordeaux

for Ciara

I lift my eyes each morning
to the aerial postcard above my desk,
from the time we flew over
to see you.
Where you've gone to roost
in a fusty attic in the russet roofs,
by the twin-spired cathedral;
two hands to heaven.

Son

for Cian

you nearly bled out from your mother,
that night on the stairs you and she bent in two;

the moon shifted, a tide resiled.

Later, you helter-skeltered out.   I eyed you
while they wiped and weighed and wrapped
and found that quirk of you;
your fingers uniquely arranged; your ring one longest

for the heart sign, the love line,
a tie to a moon surge.

The Falconer's Daughter at Twenty

for Doireann

Fly now my young eyass,
no longer bejessed.
No tinkling bell will find you;
gone the leash,
no creance even for longer
hold.
Now grown full summed,
unhooded
I trust you skywards,
in yarak,
to take the air.

In a City Garden

Lush of geranium cloy and leaf fuzz
and mother's scent of night stock.

Then the secrets to pass; the dragon that could gape,
the sour-bellied sorrel by the blue barred gate.

Rambling roses for the nuns' altar, arm-hefts of lilac dust
dark after summer's evening fall.

One fence he built of greying boards.
One fence he pliered of coat hangers.

A plate cooling in balance on the open sash window
above a long-cracked sill of granite.

Once a rabbit with the smell of a stable.
Once a mouse kept in the red boot of a tricycle.

Blade Smithing Day at Blessington Forge

Huff of the shovel in the coal bin
whoor of the fan
shhh of the flame rise.

Now
reach and draw from ranks of
rust-dusted tongs
half round   box jaw   goose-necked,
duckbilled.
Grip
the pizzle of iron
that will bear the bare blade from within.
Shish it into the piled coal caldera you have created
and leave it
but you cannot
in your newness you withdraw it and gawp
return it with a *crish* and wait
for red
and wait overlong till the forewarned
Hallowe'en sparkler stars appear
Now. Now clinker. Quake and crake it over
bed it in the slack
till it purges out to orange
then offer it to the colder altar
of the anvil and persuade it
relax under the *tok*
of your first taps
till confidence in heat and blow rising
heft the next-up hammer

slam the blank
thunk
thunk again
and over again
and over
until a patina of hollows
creeps it into the shape's pattern;
the fining, fining of the rat-tail tang
the lying down of the blade —
hunk and *hunk* and it goes
till tang and blade and tip and edge,
choil and spine
are hammered true
and done.

The whole roiled
into oil then carried
to burnish and file
to the edge.

On evenings without warning

my father took the poker
and rammed it in the kitchen fire
to start its backwards journey;
bedded there, it smithed
past starting red,
through shocking orange,
white.

Now ready, with a swathe of towel,
he inserts it in the grate bars
and pushes till it bends because it will.
Or plunges it through water's skin
to breath the ferric steam
and watch the flittering iron flakes
raining through the water.

My father hadn't control of much
but for us he could handle iron.

Rus in Suburbe

Behind a straggling chainlink fence
that winds along the motorway,

upping and downing over hummocks
of concrete and oxidised car parts,

the flock of suburban sheep graze
through the lush

thistles, the verdant nettles.
Under the branches

of a pylon they wend their way
over undulating

asbestos, the sun picking out their fleece
against the hue of the galvanising plant.

You don't mean the world to me

after Billy Collin's 'Litany'

after Jacques Crickillon's '...you are the bread and the knife...'

You are not the crystal bead on morning grass
you are not the foaming crema on my coffee
you are not the jamb of my closing door
nor the chime of my waking Mac
you are not the air that I breathe
nor my feet up on my writing desk
no post landing on the floor
really not even my cup of tea
you are no finished poem

no butterpool in the muffin
no cove in the oyster
you are no bloody
Mary
although

you are my panic
the dough rising
the daily bread
the best thing
since sliced pan

Forced March

The monotony is broken by a call
to mass. We leave *Caesar's Gallic Wars*
to line up on the metal walkway
suspended on the outside of the school.

One of the brothers patrols the line, amusing
himself by flicking at the odd boy
with his leather. The boys amuse themselves
by spitting down at the odd car when he passes.

We lurch off eventually and make our way
down the back stairs, march in good order
down the alleyway by the weeping wall of the bonded
warehouse and stagger in the narrow side door of the church.

Press-ganged into waxed pews, inhaling
the smell of sanctity and incontinence
lingering from the morning mass,
we kneel and alleluia our way

through the litany of the saints or are hauled from the depths
of examining our conscience to lift our voices in:
Réir Dé go ndéanaim agus beatha na Naomh go dtuillim.
But in the core of the phalanx, we gusto out our paraphrase:
It's a rare day for singin', and for boppin' with Bob Dylan!

The brothers call
Sing out boys! Hold the line!
And we oblige, till in the guttering light,
the saints' sorrow wavers to a smile
and the brothers glow.

Réir Dé go ndéanaim agus beatha na Naomh go dtuillim: I strive to do the will of God and earn the lives of the Saints.

City Quay 1941

Then the slow draw slow
of hawser on stanchion
and the creaking heave of the tide's ride
the edge-cut silver hacked in the iron
of the rolling gangplank.

Below in their overcoats and caps
the dockers settle themselves
for the long wind of the gantry
hobnails click and slide
on cobbled campshires
as the plimsoll line reveals
her release her hold
hatch clang, hawser strain
flume of diesel and dark
and drink.

Those who missed the cut
watch the lift and load in hopes
a slip or a break
will give them a start
from some man's finish.

The Women's Circle

The women were crocheting tiny hats

They're for little newborn babes she said
as I fingered the various caps

and picked one up, the littlest of all
This couldn't be right

I said *this wouldn't go on a toddler's fist*
it won't get used at all

Ah it will she said *some of them*
would be very small

But for someone so slight wouldn't there be
sterile hats and wraps and such?

Not something made in someone's house with
children, breakfast, dogs and TV?

Well they're not for living babies
she said *They're for dead ones*

so parents can see them nice
And she told of a newborn baby

handed over
shrouded in blue paper towels.

clear full moon
the woodpile bleak
as a block print

For All Those Who Wait for Loved Ones to Die

who pace the sea-green corridor
who wonder at the weight of time
who tread it like deep water;

this why-ing time.

Carry the weight of the room,
keep backs to time, friction feet
against the pull of marmoleum;

this wall beating time.

With every pick of cover mapped and tile-edge travelled
live in the pre-grave time
and wait for dark to pierce through;

this carapace time.

Watch.

Sit, hear and nod.
Thumb-stroke the thin envelope,
smooth the counterpane
and wait

wait

wait
and pray your waning body boxed.
Wait
— for swingeing time

to have its moment
— for the tipover
into only yesterdays of you.

go pace that sea-green corridor
go tread it like deep water

Ginger Dunning

Royal Dublin Fusiliers 1914-1918

Our grandfather John, his used face so lived and livered,
sat every day and looked out past shattered hangtrees,
by corpse-edged pools, his ragged ears still hearing
the child-cries of men for their mothers;
left right there, left in his great heavy head.

The army had a black mark or two against him;
it's said he was to transport a German prisoner
by train somewhere — where we don't know
and being required to cuff him said:
'I'll not chain any man,'
then put the other on his honour.

But could it have happened so?
Wouldn't he have been court-martialled
or it be seen in transit?
Or on and on, up and over
the fusillade of possibilities —
yet still

that small light in no man's land.

And two; the other mark
in his ear
a dark pellet of shrapnel memory
which he'd let us feel,
our soft fingers caressing sharp
smiles from his ginger 'tache.
They'd left it in — to work it loose
would have been worse.

Two marks
all the time he carried
and we remarked his life by them.

Talisman

A big country-hand made from drumlins and barbed wire,
squeezes into the bone — digging the badger of sorrow

from the deep. As if personally responsible:
'Sorry for your trouble.' He covers himself again.

Another holds your hand and bicep like a shield worn against the throng.
Delivers the long message: 'She knows all the secrets now.'

Out of the corner of his mouth to the uncle:
'Looks like they've started pullin' from our pen.'

A distant cousin: 'You'll know the meaning
of a lump in the throat now.'

Grave words; a hex against the hollowness
when a handful of earth hits it.

The Tie

i

'Hunnnk!' goes his Klaxon horn. Uncle Georgie drives up.
The house-sized *Roadmakers* gravel truck too high to come down from.
'Grushie!' we shout.
He throws the coins — among our friends we grow.

ii

'Woh Hoh! Commancheros! The Magic Tie!'
He does an Oliver Hardy fol-de-rol
with it, over his portly form.
Out from its folds peeps the tenner
my mother has just slipped in.

iii

His sister's funeral —
'Would yiz have any steak left yiz don't want?'
he says to the waitress.
'To bring home for the oul' dog?'

iv

'That man!' The Wife says, 'When he goes,
I'm going to put on his stone:
Late of the White Horse'

v

But when I look for him in his local
he's home with her.
I slip the curate a ton to cover his slate.

Haircut

You come from your new job in the pig factory early,
wash your hands again in the scullery sink.

You unroll on the table your hairdresser's roll,
tonight is the night for Uncle John's trim.

The ivory-handled razor with its French honing,
you strop carelessly across your cracked hand.

Slip your fingers in the rings of the scissors,
snip the air with them in slivers.

The thinning ones, marked *Solingen*,
with teeth like steel grass,

make a crunching sound
as you test them by your ear.

Even now, the hairs stand
on the back of my neck.

Sorting through

the last of the boxes from my mother's house;
the biscuit tin of old photographs.
Mostly, the 'man on the bridge photos'
which all Dublin families had.

A city street, my father in his twenties,
lost in a Chicago gangster overcoat;
on his arm, my mother beaming.

In another, wheeling his bike
past the Metropole Cinema,
with two young headscarfed women,
their heads turned
to gaze at him. Neither of them
are my mother.

She appears in a sepia one,
a young girl, arms linked with my grandfather.
It seems to be summer;
his gabardine drapes over his other arm,
she wears a light dress and a smile
of delight at being in town.

The same smile as in the memorial cards
we have just had printed up, a year
after her funeral.

In an early polaroid,
three elderly women sit fading
on a bench in the sun. On the back;
'Mornington 1976'.

The last time this photo surfaced,
my mother said, 'throw that out —
sure they're all dead.'
I glance at it once more
then flick it
into the waste.

Two Hours Past Midnight

and rain falls on the French isles.
By now you are far away.
Yet the distance and the time
doesn't stop me sharing
in my mind
with you
the moon on the white gables,
the rain on the Marie,
the lightning flash
further off into France,
the small window
through which
we look.

snail on the dewy wall
under the dripping fennel
its head turned back to graze

Bog Sward

Hearing
the clinkety-clink beetle
from that bog sward in the rising heat —
he lifts her
high,
high above the paths
silk-threaded and spider-strewn,
then sets her down,
down
till they are palisaded
by Timothy, Fox Sedge, Woodrush,
Melick
— the old gods.

Half earthed there,
where rushes arch over liquid jet,
they merge.

The Taxidermist Mounts the Great Crested Grebe

for the grebe in The Dead Zoo

Struggling
with the limpskin
he has drawn
from the sack,
he mock poses it
in penguin attitude,
a posing wire
from cloaca
to bill.
Disgusted, he desists.
Cat attitude then:
his hand must cup
yet flatten it into
the benchwater.
At the motes he
sneezes and spits,
sits the skin on it,
poses it in leg-trail
swim. Tilts
the ruffed head
to eye a frog they
will spy beneath it
midwater;
legs a-dangle
in poised time.

Porpoise Corpse

I found it on the Howth rocks
high from water and time

its sheet rubber skin
dull in dryness sleek in wet

its bombhead blown to the world

the water lifted then
                    the monotone flowered red

and from the charnel of its ossuary head

something reached
and pulled me outside in.

Craiceann

My skin crawls
in the middle of the night
I shiver-wake as it sloughs
off my flesh and slithers
down the bedside
across the boarded floor
by the door it slop-stands
and slaps the handle
then emptied of energy
slumps and slips through the gap.

Flayed I lie in clammy quiet
while below it roams the house
and lays itself where you have lain
it ruts the door jamb
puddles itself by the fire
drapes the arm of the sofa
like a crumpled bog-body
bone-broke and mash-faced.

It comes back then
carrying you in its rank sweat
and oozes in a shiver along me
layers you over my cold core
hoods me with its caul
I run my hands where
it creases
smooth you onto me
glove-tight.

Remember the 3030s?

Plug into it! When we said trench things like
'lube man how fraj'

And we wore our gommits outside
for all to see

And the public flailings —
the rush when you caught a piece of skin

And kranj really tasted of something then
till everyone was doing it and the quality went dube

And one time at the blessing six were chosen
the host was everywhere and they screamed
right to the end

And there was a child in the district
a human one
that was allowed
till it was eight

Field Notes on the Hedgehog

Its skull on my bookshelf —
the rank of jagged teeth more than should be needed,
in such a prickle-ball child's toy of an animal.

By night it might rear up,
a medieval machine of war, a parabellum
firing javelins drawn from its quivering body.

Or hedge snurfler, go tiggy winkling,
carrying a seething flea colony
in the cack of its undergrowth.

St Peregrine of Carcassone used one
to scarify his sores — harvesting
the ooze for the faithfuls' phials.

In her gilded chasuble she quartered
his altar, slavering crumbs of host,
to the *tic tac* of claws on marble.

Sam Whippet

For he is whippet of the race of gaze hounds.
For he is embroiled in muscle unless
he is being the cat prince ensconced
on someone else's favourite chair.

Wind is in him — he overtakes it
yet will not stir out the door to meet it.
Yet meeting it out on the green or in the wood
he will chase and turn it tearing
out his angling dew claws on his carved reverb.

Squirrels are his sworn nemesis
from some ancestral feud.
When he comes upon a drey he halloos all his kin
to its destruction till he be taken from the fray
in a writhing mass of sinew and bowstring.

Rain he will not abide on his countenance
but regally shiver till a bondservant
gives him ingress, plies him with his cloak
as he takes his throne.

dripping tap —
bamboo thriving
in the hose-ban

Paschal Watering the Garden

Two women make their way
from above the garden
wending their way down the slope.

He places his thumb over the spout
of the spigot, fluming the water, bending
to see its run-off, the carry of some dust,
the soakage into the gravel layer.

The women trill themselves through the foliage,
swathing their hair as they come, tendrils
of them moving on the air, following
their passage.

He thinks the white root network,
slow walk of the greenfly, grains
of loam in his hand webs.

The Cherry Tree

My hand moves along the snow ridge of your back
as the Friday light moves into its evening.

Each time you stir and wake me
it has slid a little more to dark.

The cherry tree's blossoms shine out.
Soon they will rain snow petals

and later the crows' bombardment
of beak-marked slippings will

thump onto the shed or lie in wait
under grass for the passing feet of summer.

But now, in the darkening Friday, my hand
curves past your hip and onwards,

as the cherry blossom begins to melt.

Elephant

Although I am here and you are there
and the ground between us gets
more and more rocky,
right here, right now,
the elephant
is not sitting in the room;
it is outside
fully tackled
to cross the Alps
and I am Hannibal
astride it.

Goldfinch

The straggled skin of the goldfinch
we fed for weeks on black seed
lay on the muddled path after the downpour.
Rain-scragged plumage dragged into quill points
each writing the quenched fire of a half bird,
the failed spark of some guttered pyre.
His tiny cape of streelish feathers
spatchcocked on the marl,
his small red mask, the peeping
wingstreak of yellow, gave off
the flittering joy he had given us.

I couldn't tell you he has gone;
just as I can't tell you we are a thing
torn in half, dragged onto
death, cold as wet ash.

spring light
the shivering ivy
spits out a wren

Memento

Our father
entertained us
in graveyards;
Sunday morning,
the vaults of the rich.
Squat granite blockhouses
ranked along the sidewall.
Multiple skins of green paint
over amorphous coats of arms.
Receding tracery of light
through the grilles,
the particular beauty of dust
lit by stained glass,
over the cryptic slump
of leaden caskets.
Two small boys wide-eyed
at a vase of sear flowers
unexplained.

Tearaways

It was the only time I wished my father would beat us.
We had run away, my brother and I to the far reaches
of the edge of our neighbourhood and we crouched
hugging our knees to our chins behind the canal wall.

The canal water fell. Trucks rumbled over the bridge.
Clouds passed. We went on huddling.
His head appeared over the parapet and he said —
nothing. My brother looked to me.
I wanted so badly to speak but some weight
was on me and no words fit.

He lifted my brother to the crossbar of his bike,
motioned me to the back carrier
and we wobbled home.

Raft Making

It's like as kids; we played
with ice-pop sticks
making 'rafts' with them —

first a square, next cross-spars
to make a window
then the final pieces
gingerly flexing,
nervously inserting.
Until at last you pushed
too much
and the chance of
something perfectly
holding

sprung   apart

in a moment.

But occasionally we
manage to contain
the strains
and hold perfection

taut
in our hands.

My Brother Helped a Tree Up

one day as we were wandering
along the Grand Canal.

Not long planted,
it had veered off course
or fallen in the urban battle
of *gurrier* versus *civium*.

Up he shoved it against its stake
and like Cúchulainn strapped it
so it took off

over years
till it stretched out and up
with the brother but beyond
even his great girth and poll.

Long past the days
we wandered by
in *pinkeen* search,

nets and bottles ready
past blanketweed,
stuttering waterboatmen,
small creatures testing the meniscus.

Dipper

yes i could be a stone turner or a mud prober but
i prefer to be the millrace runner.
it amuses me to wander down
to the live edge of the river
and to keep on wandering
never breaking my stride
— a living bathysphere
submerging to the water
gobbets of quicksilver
fall from my back.
i — river walker
bubble maker
whitewater
sepia
robin.

Fishing in the Dark

He said, ‘let it sink through the black’.
He slipped the bail arm on his reel —
the lead weight plopped through the oily skin
of the canal basin.
The glint of the dragged line in the streetlamp
showed the sinker still travelling.
A bus passed over the swivel bridge above us,
its lights ghosting across the empty mill buildings.
In its wake, the exhaust mixed with the weedy slop of water.

‘Of course, we might get nothing,’ he said.
‘Though this time of evening is good for the eels.’
My pale grip quivered the top of my rod. He glanced
at it and me, then turned away.
‘But when we do, have your bit of sacking
ready and grab it behind its head.’
From the corner of my eye I watched my sacking
drifting out of the pool of light.
‘Mind the teeth,’ he clacked through his loose mouth.
‘Their teeth are the absolute bastard.’
He gobbed into the black, then pucked me in the shoulder
sending me sideways. ‘But with a bit of luck
you’ll only catch a small one.’

Leave Taking

September, and her house nearly clear.
Successive visits of sorting, packing,
charity shops, recycling, dump.
Finding her in chains of necklaces,
hangars of blouses and dresses.
Handmarks on doors from midnight
wanderings, screw holes from handrails,
shadow of the stairlift.
Bouquets of flowers in the windows,
their plastic petals needing a Flash rinse.
On the bare dresser; St Anthony,
now headless, jars of change, a passport
used for the funeral of her last sister.
The pair of them, thick as sisters, beam
from the sole remaining photo
sellotaped to the fridge.

With no bread bin for the backdoor key,
toss it on the empty dresser.
Pull the door behind you.

And that time will curtain

and we will draw it
from the other side to hang
lightly moving in an olive wind

and postcard-blue doors
open to cool dark
show glimpses of *marché* tablecloths
and paint crusted chair legs

and the plainest pitcher of thin local wine
run pine, lavender and salt air
on our tongues

while fingers link momentarily
then release as the swell ebbs
and the taut hooks ease.

Acknowledgements & Thanks

Acknowledgements are due to the editors of the following publications and media where some of the poems here, or versions of them, first appeared:

Crannóg, Southword, Cork Community Radio, Dublin South FM, The Irish Times, Flare, Revival, Poetry Ireland Review, Skylight 47, Cyphers, Between the Leaves–New Haiku Writing from Ireland, The Stony Thursday Book, Dodging the Rain, Ropes (UCG), *The Shotglass Journal, Stinging Fly, Magma, The French Literary Review, Fields Journal* (University of Texas at Austin), *Blithe Spirit, Live Encounters,* and *The Well Review.*

*

My thanks to the Arts Office South Dublin County Council for a Tyrone Guthrie Centre residency and Words Ireland Mentoring Award. Bualadh bos to the Irish Writers' Centre for numerous courses and space to write.

A deep bow to those who have encouraged and supported my writing along the way; my fellow writers in the Scurrilous Squirrels Writers' group; Gavan Duffy, Maria Kenny, Katie Martin, Jonathan Saint — may your knives never blunt. Likewise the Quarterman men — it's a quare name but great stuff from Daragh Bradish, Seamus Cashman and Tom Conaty. To numerous teachers, encouragers, listeners and influencers in the true sense of the word but particularly Joan Nevin, Yvonne Cullen, Jean O'Brien, Nuala O'Connor, Enda Wyley, Sean O'Connor. My thanks to Jonathan Saint for proofreading.

Special thanks to Jessie Lendennie and Siobhán Hutson Jeanotte for getting us there through interesting times.

Awefull appreciation to Sally Caulwell for the glorious cover art.

And my deepest bow to the rock of my family both present and watching.

PAUL BREGAZZI was born and bred in Dublin. His poetry has been published, broadcast and anthologised widely and has been awarded and shortlisted in numerous competitions including: Rialto Nature, the Bridport, Bailieborough, Ledwidge, Magma Editor's Prize, Touchstone Haiku of the Year (U.S.) and the Genjuan International Haibun Competition (Japan). He was selected for Poetry Ireland's Introduction Series in 2015 and won the Cúirt New Writing Prize for Poetry 2017. He is a member of the four-man collaborative collective Quarterman, was a co-founder with Daragh Bradish of the Listeners literary group and serves as an Assistant Editor with *The Haibun Journal.* He was the recipient of a South Dublin Co. Council Tyrone Guthrie Centre residency in 2018 and the Words Ireland Mentorship programme in 2019. He received an Arts Council Agility Award in 2023.

salmonpoetry

Cliffs of Moher, County Clare, Ireland

'Publishing the finest Irish and international literature.'

Michael D. Higgins, President of Ireland